If found, please return to

E D I T I O N

THATSPPTISH

Illustrated Journals and Gifts by Priyanka Paul Tiwari

WWW.THATSPPTISH.COM

Keep it Safe

Keep it Close

USEFUL AT-A-GLANCE INFORMATION

Internet Service Provider :

Account Number :

Customer Service :

Broadband :

Username :   Password :

Wireless 1 :

Username :   Password :

Wireless 2 :

Username :   Password :

My Email (personal) :

Password :

My Email (work) :

Password :

My Email (business) :

Password :

HELLO

IMPORTANT CONTACTS

Name
_____

Relation
_____

E-mail
_____

Phone
_____

Name
_____

Relation
_____

E-mail
_____

Phone
_____

Name
_____

Relation
_____

E-mail
_____

Phone
_____

Name
_____

Relation
_____

E-mail
_____

Phone
_____

Name
_____

Relation
_____

E-mail
_____

Phone
_____

IMPORTANT CONTACTS

Name

Relation

E-mail

Phone

Name

Relation

E-mail

Phone

Name

Relation

E-mail

Phone

Name

Relation

E-mail

Phone

Name

Relation

E-mail

Phone

IMPORTANT CONTACTS

Name

Relation

E-mail

Phone

Name

Relation

E-mail

Phone

Name

Relation

E-mail

Phone

Name

Relation

E-mail

Phone

Name

Relation

E-mail

Phone

A

WEBSITE

USERNAME

PASSWORD

E-MAIL USED

NOTES

WEBSITE

USERNAME

PASSWORD

E-MAIL USED

NOTES

WEBSITE

USERNAME

PASSWORD

E-MAIL USED

NOTES

WEBSITE

USERNAME

PASSWORD

E-MAIL USED

NOTES

A

WEBSITE

USERNAME

PASSWORD

E-MAIL USED

NOTES

WEBSITE

USERNAME

PASSWORD

E-MAIL USED

NOTES

WEBSITE

USERNAME

PASSWORD

E-MAIL USED

NOTES

WEBSITE

USERNAME

PASSWORD

E-MAIL USED

NOTES

A

WEBSITE

USERNAME

PASSWORD

E-MAIL USED

NOTES

WEBSITE

USERNAME

PASSWORD

E-MAIL USED

NOTES

WEBSITE

USERNAME

PASSWORD

E-MAIL USED

NOTES

WEBSITE

USERNAME

PASSWORD

E-MAIL USED

NOTES

A

WEBSITE

USERNAME

PASSWORD

E-MAIL USED

NOTES

WEBSITE

USERNAME

PASSWORD

E-MAIL USED

NOTES

WEBSITE

USERNAME

PASSWORD

E-MAIL USED

NOTES

WEBSITE

USERNAME

PASSWORD

E-MAIL USED

NOTES

B

WEBSITE

USERNAME

PASSWORD

E-MAIL USED

NOTES

WEBSITE

USERNAME

PASSWORD

E-MAIL USED

NOTES

WEBSITE

USERNAME

PASSWORD

E-MAIL USED

NOTES

WEBSITE

USERNAME

PASSWORD

E-MAIL USED

NOTES

B

WEBSITE

USERNAME

PASSWORD

E-MAIL USED

NOTES

WEBSITE

USERNAME

PASSWORD

E-MAIL USED

NOTES

WEBSITE

USERNAME

PASSWORD

E-MAIL USED

NOTES

WEBSITE

USERNAME

PASSWORD

E-MAIL USED

NOTES

B

WEBSITE

USERNAME

PASSWORD

E-MAIL USED

NOTES

WEBSITE

USERNAME

PASSWORD

E-MAIL USED

NOTES

WEBSITE

USERNAME

PASSWORD

E-MAIL USED

NOTES

WEBSITE

USERNAME

PASSWORD

E-MAIL USED

NOTES

WEBSITE

USERNAME

PASSWORD

E-MAIL USED

NOTES

WEBSITE

USERNAME

PASSWORD

E-MAIL USED

NOTES

WEBSITE

USERNAME

PASSWORD

E-MAIL USED

NOTES

WEBSITE

USERNAME

PASSWORD

E-MAIL USED

NOTES

C

WEBSITE

USERNAME

PASSWORD

E-MAIL USED

NOTES

WEBSITE

USERNAME

PASSWORD

E-MAIL USED

NOTES

WEBSITE

USERNAME

PASSWORD

E-MAIL USED

NOTES

WEBSITE

USERNAME

PASSWORD

E-MAIL USED

NOTES

WEBSITE

USERNAME

PASSWORD

E-MAIL USED

NOTES

WEBSITE

USERNAME

PASSWORD

E-MAIL USED

NOTES

WEBSITE

USERNAME

PASSWORD

E-MAIL USED

NOTES

WEBSITE

USERNAME

PASSWORD

E-MAIL USED

NOTES

C

WEBSITE

USERNAME

PASSWORD

E-MAIL USED

NOTES

WEBSITE

USERNAME

PASSWORD

E-MAIL USED

NOTES

WEBSITE

USERNAME

PASSWORD

E-MAIL USED

NOTES

WEBSITE

USERNAME

PASSWORD

E-MAIL USED

NOTES

WEBSITE

USERNAME

PASSWORD

E-MAIL USED

NOTES

WEBSITE

USERNAME

PASSWORD

E-MAIL USED

NOTES

WEBSITE

USERNAME

PASSWORD

E-MAIL USED

NOTES

WEBSITE

USERNAME

PASSWORD

E-MAIL USED

NOTES

D

WEBSITE

USERNAME

PASSWORD

E-MAIL USED

NOTES

WEBSITE

USERNAME

PASSWORD

E-MAIL USED

NOTES

WEBSITE

USERNAME

PASSWORD

E-MAIL USED

NOTES

WEBSITE

USERNAME

PASSWORD

E-MAIL USED

NOTES

D

WEBSITE

USERNAME

PASSWORD

E-MAIL USED

NOTES

WEBSITE

USERNAME

PASSWORD

E-MAIL USED

NOTES

WEBSITE

USERNAME

PASSWORD

E-MAIL USED

NOTES

WEBSITE

USERNAME

PASSWORD

E-MAIL USED

NOTES

WEBSITE

USERNAME

PASSWORD

E-MAIL USED

NOTES

WEBSITE

USERNAME

PASSWORD

E-MAIL USED

NOTES

WEBSITE

USERNAME

PASSWORD

E-MAIL USED

NOTES

WEBSITE

USERNAME

PASSWORD

E-MAIL USED

NOTES

E

WEBSITE

USERNAME

PASSWORD

E-MAIL USED

NOTES

WEBSITE

USERNAME

PASSWORD

E-MAIL USED

NOTES

WEBSITE

USERNAME

PASSWORD

E-MAIL USED

NOTES

WEBSITE

USERNAME

PASSWORD

E-MAIL USED

NOTES

WEBSITE

USERNAME

PASSWORD

E-MAIL USED

NOTES

WEBSITE

USERNAME

PASSWORD

E-MAIL USED

NOTES

WEBSITE

USERNAME

PASSWORD

E-MAIL USED

NOTES

WEBSITE

USERNAME

PASSWORD

E-MAIL USED

NOTES

WEBSITE

USERNAME

PASSWORD

E-MAIL USED

NOTES

WEBSITE

USERNAME

PASSWORD

E-MAIL USED

NOTES

WEBSITE

USERNAME

PASSWORD

E-MAIL USED

NOTES

WEBSITE

USERNAME

PASSWORD

E-MAIL USED

NOTES

F

WEBSITE

USERNAME

PASSWORD

E-MAIL USED

NOTES

WEBSITE

USERNAME

PASSWORD

E-MAIL USED

NOTES

WEBSITE

USERNAME

PASSWORD

E-MAIL USED

NOTES

WEBSITE

USERNAME

PASSWORD

E-MAIL USED

NOTES

WEBSITE

USERNAME

PASSWORD

E-MAIL USED

NOTES

WEBSITE

USERNAME

PASSWORD

E-MAIL USED

NOTES

WEBSITE

USERNAME

PASSWORD

E-MAIL USED

NOTES

WEBSITE

USERNAME

PASSWORD

E-MAIL USED

NOTES

F

WEBSITE

USERNAME

PASSWORD

E-MAIL USED

NOTES

WEBSITE

USERNAME

PASSWORD

E-MAIL USED

NOTES

WEBSITE

USERNAME

PASSWORD

E-MAIL USED

NOTES

WEBSITE

USERNAME

PASSWORD

E-MAIL USED

NOTES

F

WEBSITE

USERNAME

PASSWORD

E-MAIL USED

NOTES

WEBSITE

USERNAME

PASSWORD

E-MAIL USED

NOTES

WEBSITE

USERNAME

PASSWORD

E-MAIL USED

NOTES

WEBSITE

USERNAME

PASSWORD

E-MAIL USED

NOTES

G

WEBSITE

USERNAME

PASSWORD

E-MAIL USED

NOTES

WEBSITE

USERNAME

PASSWORD

E-MAIL USED

NOTES

WEBSITE

USERNAME

PASSWORD

E-MAIL USED

NOTES

WEBSITE

USERNAME

PASSWORD

E-MAIL USED

NOTES

WEBSITE

USERNAME

PASSWORD

E-MAIL USED

NOTES

WEBSITE

USERNAME

PASSWORD

E-MAIL USED

NOTES

WEBSITE

USERNAME

PASSWORD

E-MAIL USED

NOTES

WEBSITE

USERNAME

PASSWORD

E-MAIL USED

NOTES

G

WEBSITE

USERNAME

PASSWORD

E-MAIL USED

NOTES

WEBSITE

USERNAME

PASSWORD

E-MAIL USED

NOTES

WEBSITE

USERNAME

PASSWORD

E-MAIL USED

NOTES

WEBSITE

USERNAME

PASSWORD

E-MAIL USED

NOTES

G

WEBSITE

USERNAME

PASSWORD

E-MAIL USED

NOTES

WEBSITE

USERNAME

PASSWORD

E-MAIL USED

NOTES

WEBSITE

USERNAME

PASSWORD

E-MAIL USED

NOTES

WEBSITE

USERNAME

PASSWORD

E-MAIL USED

NOTES

H

WEBSITE

USERNAME

PASSWORD

E-MAIL USED

NOTES

WEBSITE

USERNAME

PASSWORD

E-MAIL USED

NOTES

WEBSITE

USERNAME

PASSWORD

E-MAIL USED

NOTES

WEBSITE

USERNAME

PASSWORD

E-MAIL USED

NOTES

WEBSITE

USERNAME

PASSWORD

E-MAIL USED

NOTES

WEBSITE

USERNAME

PASSWORD

E-MAIL USED

NOTES

WEBSITE

USERNAME

PASSWORD

E-MAIL USED

NOTES

WEBSITE

USERNAME

PASSWORD

E-MAIL USED

NOTES

WEBSITE

USERNAME

PASSWORD

E-MAIL USED

NOTES

WEBSITE

USERNAME

PASSWORD

E-MAIL USED

NOTES

WEBSITE

USERNAME

PASSWORD

E-MAIL USED

NOTES

WEBSITE

USERNAME

PASSWORD

E-MAIL USED

NOTES

H

WEBSITE

USERNAME

PASSWORD

E-MAIL USED

NOTES

WEBSITE

USERNAME

PASSWORD

E-MAIL USED

NOTES

WEBSITE

USERNAME

PASSWORD

E-MAIL USED

NOTES

WEBSITE

USERNAME

PASSWORD

E-MAIL USED

NOTES

I

WEBSITE

USERNAME

PASSWORD

E-MAIL USED

NOTES

WEBSITE

USERNAME

PASSWORD

E-MAIL USED

NOTES

WEBSITE

USERNAME

PASSWORD

E-MAIL USED

NOTES

WEBSITE

USERNAME

PASSWORD

E-MAIL USED

NOTES

WEBSITE

USERNAME

PASSWORD

E-MAIL USED

NOTES

WEBSITE

USERNAME

PASSWORD

E-MAIL USED

NOTES

WEBSITE

USERNAME

PASSWORD

E-MAIL USED

NOTES

WEBSITE

USERNAME

PASSWORD

E-MAIL USED

NOTES

I

WEBSITE

USERNAME

PASSWORD

E-MAIL USED

NOTES

WEBSITE

USERNAME

PASSWORD

E-MAIL USED

NOTES

WEBSITE

USERNAME

PASSWORD

E-MAIL USED

NOTES

WEBSITE

USERNAME

PASSWORD

E-MAIL USED

NOTES

I

WEBSITE

USERNAME

PASSWORD

E-MAIL USED

NOTES

WEBSITE

USERNAME

PASSWORD

E-MAIL USED

NOTES

WEBSITE

USERNAME

PASSWORD

E-MAIL USED

NOTES

WEBSITE

USERNAME

PASSWORD

E-MAIL USED

NOTES

J

WEBSITE

USERNAME

PASSWORD

E-MAIL USED

NOTES

WEBSITE

USERNAME

PASSWORD

E-MAIL USED

NOTES

WEBSITE

USERNAME

PASSWORD

E-MAIL USED

NOTES

WEBSITE

USERNAME

PASSWORD

E-MAIL USED

NOTES

J

WEBSITE

USERNAME

PASSWORD

E-MAIL USED

NOTES

WEBSITE

USERNAME

PASSWORD

E-MAIL USED

NOTES

WEBSITE

USERNAME

PASSWORD

E-MAIL USED

NOTES

WEBSITE

USERNAME

PASSWORD

E-MAIL USED

NOTES

J

WEBSITE

USERNAME

PASSWORD

E-MAIL USED

NOTES

WEBSITE

USERNAME

PASSWORD

E-MAIL USED

NOTES

WEBSITE

USERNAME

PASSWORD

E-MAIL USED

NOTES

WEBSITE

USERNAME

PASSWORD

E-MAIL USED

NOTES

J

WEBSITE

USERNAME

PASSWORD

E-MAIL USED

NOTES

WEBSITE

USERNAME

PASSWORD

E-MAIL USED

NOTES

WEBSITE

USERNAME

PASSWORD

E-MAIL USED

NOTES

WEBSITE

USERNAME

PASSWORD

E-MAIL USED

NOTES

WEBSITE

USERNAME

PASSWORD

E-MAIL USED

NOTES

WEBSITE

USERNAME

PASSWORD

E-MAIL USED

NOTES

WEBSITE

USERNAME

PASSWORD

E-MAIL USED

NOTES

WEBSITE

USERNAME

PASSWORD

E-MAIL USED

NOTES

WEBSITE

USERNAME

PASSWORD

E-MAIL USED

NOTES

WEBSITE

USERNAME

PASSWORD

E-MAIL USED

NOTES

WEBSITE

USERNAME

PASSWORD

E-MAIL USED

NOTES

WEBSITE

USERNAME

PASSWORD

E-MAIL USED

NOTES

K

WEBSITE

USERNAME

PASSWORD

E-MAIL USED

NOTES

WEBSITE

USERNAME

PASSWORD

E-MAIL USED

NOTES

WEBSITE

USERNAME

PASSWORD

E-MAIL USED

NOTES

WEBSITE

USERNAME

PASSWORD

E-MAIL USED

NOTES

WEBSITE

USERNAME

PASSWORD

E-MAIL USED

NOTES

WEBSITE

USERNAME

PASSWORD

E-MAIL USED

NOTES

WEBSITE

USERNAME

PASSWORD

E-MAIL USED

NOTES

WEBSITE

USERNAME

PASSWORD

E-MAIL USED

NOTES

L

WEBSITE

USERNAME

PASSWORD

E-MAIL USED

NOTES

WEBSITE

USERNAME

PASSWORD

E-MAIL USED

NOTES

WEBSITE

USERNAME

PASSWORD

E-MAIL USED

NOTES

WEBSITE

USERNAME

PASSWORD

E-MAIL USED

NOTES

L

WEBSITE

USERNAME

PASSWORD

E-MAIL USED

NOTES

WEBSITE

USERNAME

PASSWORD

E-MAIL USED

NOTES

WEBSITE

USERNAME

PASSWORD

E-MAIL USED

NOTES

WEBSITE

USERNAME

PASSWORD

E-MAIL USED

NOTES

L

WEBSITE

USERNAME

PASSWORD

E-MAIL USED

NOTES

WEBSITE

USERNAME

PASSWORD

E-MAIL USED

NOTES

WEBSITE

USERNAME

PASSWORD

E-MAIL USED

NOTES

WEBSITE

USERNAME

PASSWORD

E-MAIL USED

NOTES

WEBSITE

USERNAME

PASSWORD

E-MAIL USED

NOTES

WEBSITE

USERNAME

PASSWORD

E-MAIL USED

NOTES

WEBSITE

USERNAME

PASSWORD

E-MAIL USED

NOTES

WEBSITE

USERNAME

PASSWORD

E-MAIL USED

NOTES

WEBSITE

USERNAME

PASSWORD

E-MAIL USED

NOTES

WEBSITE

USERNAME

PASSWORD

E-MAIL USED

NOTES

WEBSITE

USERNAME

PASSWORD

E-MAIL USED

NOTES

WEBSITE

USERNAME

PASSWORD

E-MAIL USED

NOTES

WEBSITE

USERNAME

PASSWORD

E-MAIL USED

NOTES

WEBSITE

USERNAME

PASSWORD

E-MAIL USED

NOTES

WEBSITE

USERNAME

PASSWORD

E-MAIL USED

NOTES

WEBSITE

USERNAME

PASSWORD

E-MAIL USED

NOTES

N

WEBSITE

USERNAME

PASSWORD

E-MAIL USED

NOTES

WEBSITE

USERNAME

PASSWORD

E-MAIL USED

NOTES

WEBSITE

USERNAME

PASSWORD

E-MAIL USED

NOTES

WEBSITE

USERNAME

PASSWORD

E-MAIL USED

NOTES

N

WEBSITE

USERNAME

PASSWORD

E-MAIL USED

NOTES

WEBSITE

USERNAME

PASSWORD

E-MAIL USED

NOTES

WEBSITE

USERNAME

PASSWORD

E-MAIL USED

NOTES

WEBSITE

USERNAME

PASSWORD

E-MAIL USED

NOTES

WEBSITE

USERNAME

PASSWORD

E-MAIL USED

NOTES

WEBSITE

USERNAME

PASSWORD

E-MAIL USED

NOTES

WEBSITE

USERNAME

PASSWORD

E-MAIL USED

NOTES

WEBSITE

USERNAME

PASSWORD

E-MAIL USED

NOTES

WEBSITE

USERNAME

PASSWORD

EMAIL USED

NOTES

WEBSITE

USERNAME

PASSWORD

EMAIL USED

NOTES

WEBSITE

USERNAME

PASSWORD

EMAIL USED

NOTES

WEBSITE

USERNAME

PASSWORD

EMAIL USED

NOTES

N

WEBSITE

USERNAME

PASSWORD

E-MAIL USED

NOTES

WEBSITE

USERNAME

PASSWORD

E-MAIL USED

NOTES

WEBSITE

USERNAME

PASSWORD

E-MAIL USED

NOTES

WEBSITE

USERNAME

PASSWORD

E-MAIL USED

NOTES

WEBSITE

USERNAME

PASSWORD

EMAIL USED

NOTES

WEBSITE

USERNAME

PASSWORD

EMAIL USED

NOTES

WEBSITE

USERNAME

PASSWORD

EMAIL USED

NOTES

WEBSITE

USERNAME

PASSWORD

EMAIL USED

NOTES

O

WEBSITE

USERNAME

PASSWORD

E-MAIL USED

NOTES

WEBSITE

USERNAME

PASSWORD

E-MAIL USED

NOTES

WEBSITE

USERNAME

PASSWORD

E-MAIL USED

NOTES

WEBSITE

USERNAME

PASSWORD

E-MAIL USED

NOTES

O

WEBSITE

USERNAME

PASSWORD

EMAIL USED

NOTES

WEBSITE

USERNAME

PASSWORD

EMAIL USED

NOTES

WEBSITE

USERNAME

PASSWORD

EMAIL USED

NOTES

WEBSITE

USERNAME

PASSWORD

EMAIL USED

NOTES

O

WEBSITE

USERNAME

PASSWORD

E-MAIL USED

NOTES

WEBSITE

USERNAME

PASSWORD

E-MAIL USED

NOTES

WEBSITE

USERNAME

PASSWORD

E-MAIL USED

NOTES

WEBSITE

USERNAME

PASSWORD

E-MAIL USED

NOTES

WEBSITE

USERNAME

PASSWORD

E-MAIL USED

NOTES

WEBSITE

USERNAME

PASSWORD

E-MAIL USED

NOTES

WEBSITE

USERNAME

PASSWORD

E-MAIL USED

NOTES

WEBSITE

USERNAME

PASSWORD

E-MAIL USED

NOTES

P

WEBSITE

USERNAME

PASSWORD

E-MAIL USED

NOTES

WEBSITE

USERNAME

PASSWORD

E-MAIL USED

NOTES

WEBSITE

USERNAME

PASSWORD

E-MAIL USED

NOTES

WEBSITE

USERNAME

PASSWORD

E-MAIL USED

NOTES

WEBSITE

USERNAME

PASSWORD

E-MAIL USED

NOTES

WEBSITE

USERNAME

PASSWORD

E-MAIL USED

NOTES

WEBSITE

USERNAME

PASSWORD

E-MAIL USED

NOTES

WEBSITE

USERNAME

PASSWORD

E-MAIL USED

NOTES

P

WEBSITE

USERNAME

PASSWORD

E-MAIL USED

NOTES

WEBSITE

USERNAME

PASSWORD

E-MAIL USED

NOTES

WEBSITE

USERNAME

PASSWORD

E-MAIL USED

NOTES

WEBSITE

USERNAME

PASSWORD

E-MAIL USED

NOTES

WEBSITE

USERNAME

PASSWORD

E-MAIL USED

NOTES

WEBSITE

USERNAME

PASSWORD

E-MAIL USED

NOTES

WEBSITE

USERNAME

PASSWORD

E-MAIL USED

NOTES

WEBSITE

USERNAME

PASSWORD

E-MAIL USED

NOTES

Q

WEBSITE

USERNAME

PASSWORD

E-MAIL USED

NOTES

WEBSITE

USERNAME

PASSWORD

E-MAIL USED

NOTES

WEBSITE

USERNAME

PASSWORD

E-MAIL USED

NOTES

WEBSITE

USERNAME

PASSWORD

E-MAIL USED

NOTES

WEBSITE

USERNAME

PASSWORD

EMAIL USED

NOTES

WEBSITE

USERNAME

PASSWORD

EMAIL USED

NOTES

WEBSITE

USERNAME

PASSWORD

EMAIL USED

NOTES

WEBSITE

USERNAME

PASSWORD

EMAIL USED

NOTES

Q

WEBSITE

USERNAME

PASSWORD

E-MAIL USED

NOTES

WEBSITE

USERNAME

PASSWORD

E-MAIL USED

NOTES

WEBSITE

USERNAME

PASSWORD

E-MAIL USED

NOTES

WEBSITE

USERNAME

PASSWORD

E-MAIL USED

NOTES

Q

WEBSITE

USERNAME

PASSWORD

E-MAIL USED

NOTES

WEBSITE

USERNAME

PASSWORD

E-MAIL USED

NOTES

WEBSITE

USERNAME

PASSWORD

E-MAIL USED

NOTES

WEBSITE

USERNAME

PASSWORD

E-MAIL USED

NOTES

R

WEBSITE

USERNAME

PASSWORD

E-MAIL USED

NOTES

WEBSITE

USERNAME

PASSWORD

E-MAIL USED

NOTES

WEBSITE

USERNAME

PASSWORD

E-MAIL USED

NOTES

WEBSITE

USERNAME

PASSWORD

E-MAIL USED

NOTES

WEBSITE

USERNAME

PASSWORD

E-MAIL USED

NOTES

WEBSITE

USERNAME

PASSWORD

E-MAIL USED

NOTES

WEBSITE

USERNAME

PASSWORD

E-MAIL USED

NOTES

WEBSITE

USERNAME

PASSWORD

E-MAIL USED

NOTES

R

WEBSITE

USERNAME

PASSWORD

E-MAIL USED

NOTES

WEBSITE

USERNAME

PASSWORD

E-MAIL USED

NOTES

WEBSITE

USERNAME

PASSWORD

E-MAIL USED

NOTES

WEBSITE

USERNAME

PASSWORD

E-MAIL USED

NOTES

R

WEBSITE

USERNAME

PASSWORD

E-MAIL USED

NOTES

WEBSITE

USERNAME

PASSWORD

E-MAIL USED

NOTES

WEBSITE

USERNAME

PASSWORD

E-MAIL USED

NOTES

WEBSITE

USERNAME

PASSWORD

E-MAIL USED

NOTES

S

WEBSITE

USERNAME

PASSWORD

E-MAIL USED

NOTES

WEBSITE

USERNAME

PASSWORD

E-MAIL USED

NOTES

WEBSITE

USERNAME

PASSWORD

E-MAIL USED

NOTES

WEBSITE

USERNAME

PASSWORD

E-MAIL USED

NOTES

WEBSITE

USERNAME

PASSWORD

EMAIL USED

NOTES

WEBSITE

USERNAME

PASSWORD

EMAIL USED

NOTES

WEBSITE

USERNAME

PASSWORD

EMAIL USED

NOTES

WEBSITE

USERNAME

PASSWORD

EMAIL USED

NOTES

S

WEBSITE

USERNAME

PASSWORD

E-MAIL USED

NOTES

WEBSITE

USERNAME

PASSWORD

E-MAIL USED

NOTES

WEBSITE

USERNAME

PASSWORD

E-MAIL USED

NOTES

WEBSITE

USERNAME

PASSWORD

E-MAIL USED

NOTES

S

WEBSITE

USERNAME

PASSWORD

EMAIL USED

NOTES

WEBSITE

USERNAME

PASSWORD

EMAIL USED

NOTES

WEBSITE

USERNAME

PASSWORD

EMAIL USED

NOTES

WEBSITE

USERNAME

PASSWORD

EMAIL USED

NOTES

T

WEBSITE

USERNAME

PASSWORD

E-MAIL USED

NOTES

WEBSITE

USERNAME

PASSWORD

E-MAIL USED

NOTES

WEBSITE

USERNAME

PASSWORD

E-MAIL USED

NOTES

WEBSITE

USERNAME

PASSWORD

E-MAIL USED

NOTES

WEBSITE

USERNAME

PASSWORD

EMAIL USED

NOTES

WEBSITE

USERNAME

PASSWORD

EMAIL USED

NOTES

WEBSITE

USERNAME

PASSWORD

EMAIL USED

NOTES

WEBSITE

USERNAME

PASSWORD

EMAIL USED

NOTES

T

WEBSITE

USERNAME

PASSWORD

E-MAIL USED

NOTES

WEBSITE

USERNAME

PASSWORD

E-MAIL USED

NOTES

WEBSITE

USERNAME

PASSWORD

E-MAIL USED

NOTES

WEBSITE

USERNAME

PASSWORD

E-MAIL USED

NOTES

WEBSITE

USERNAME

PASSWORD

EMAIL USED

NOTES

WEBSITE

USERNAME

PASSWORD

EMAIL USED

NOTES

WEBSITE

USERNAME

PASSWORD

EMAIL USED

NOTES

WEBSITE

USERNAME

PASSWORD

EMAIL USED

NOTES

U

WEBSITE

USERNAME

PASSWORD

E-MAIL USED

NOTES

WEBSITE

USERNAME

PASSWORD

E-MAIL USED

NOTES

WEBSITE

USERNAME

PASSWORD

E-MAIL USED

NOTES

WEBSITE

USERNAME

PASSWORD

E-MAIL USED

NOTES

WEBSITE

USERNAME

PASSWORD

EMAIL USED

NOTES

WEBSITE

USERNAME

PASSWORD

EMAIL USED

NOTES

WEBSITE

USERNAME

PASSWORD

EMAIL USED

NOTES

WEBSITE

USERNAME

PASSWORD

EMAIL USED

NOTES

U

WEBSITE

USERNAME

PASSWORD

E-MAIL USED

NOTES

WEBSITE

USERNAME

PASSWORD

E-MAIL USED

NOTES

WEBSITE

USERNAME

PASSWORD

E-MAIL USED

NOTES

WEBSITE

USERNAME

PASSWORD

E-MAIL USED

NOTES

U

WEBSITE

USERNAME

PASSWORD

EMAIL USED

NOTES

WEBSITE

USERNAME

PASSWORD

EMAIL USED

NOTES

WEBSITE

USERNAME

PASSWORD

EMAIL USED

NOTES

WEBSITE

USERNAME

PASSWORD

EMAIL USED

NOTES

V

WEBSITE

USERNAME

PASSWORD

E-MAIL USED

NOTES

WEBSITE

USERNAME

PASSWORD

E-MAIL USED

NOTES

WEBSITE

USERNAME

PASSWORD

E-MAIL USED

NOTES

WEBSITE

USERNAME

PASSWORD

E-MAIL USED

NOTES

WEBSITE

USERNAME

PASSWORD

EMAIL USED

NOTES

WEBSITE

USERNAME

PASSWORD

EMAIL USED

NOTES

WEBSITE

USERNAME

PASSWORD

EMAIL USED

NOTES

WEBSITE

USERNAME

PASSWORD

EMAIL USED

NOTES

V

WEBSITE

USERNAME

PASSWORD

E-MAIL USED

NOTES

WEBSITE

USERNAME

PASSWORD

E-MAIL USED

NOTES

WEBSITE

USERNAME

PASSWORD

E-MAIL USED

NOTES

WEBSITE

USERNAME

PASSWORD

E-MAIL USED

NOTES

V

WEBSITE

USERNAME

PASSWORD

EMAIL USED

NOTES

WEBSITE

USERNAME

PASSWORD

EMAIL USED

NOTES

WEBSITE

USERNAME

PASSWORD

EMAIL USED

NOTES

WEBSITE

USERNAME

PASSWORD

EMAIL USED

NOTES

WEBSITE

USERNAME

PASSWORD

E-MAIL USED

NOTES

WEBSITE

USERNAME

PASSWORD

E-MAIL USED

NOTES

WEBSITE

USERNAME

PASSWORD

E-MAIL USED

NOTES

WEBSITE

USERNAME

PASSWORD

E-MAIL USED

NOTES

WEBSITE

USERNAME

PASSWORD

EMAIL USED

NOTES

WEBSITE

USERNAME

PASSWORD

EMAIL USED

NOTES

WEBSITE

USERNAME

PASSWORD

EMAIL USED

NOTES

WEBSITE

USERNAME

PASSWORD

EMAIL USED

NOTES

WEBSITE

USERNAME

PASSWORD

E-MAIL USED

NOTES

WEBSITE

USERNAME

PASSWORD

E-MAIL USED

NOTES

WEBSITE

USERNAME

PASSWORD

E-MAIL USED

NOTES

WEBSITE

USERNAME

PASSWORD

E-MAIL USED

NOTES

W

WEBSITE

USERNAME

PASSWORD

EMAIL USED

NOTES

WEBSITE

USERNAME

PASSWORD

EMAIL USED

NOTES

WEBSITE

USERNAME

PASSWORD

EMAIL USED

NOTES

WEBSITE

USERNAME

PASSWORD

EMAIL USED

NOTES

X

WEBSITE

USERNAME

PASSWORD

E-MAIL USED

NOTES

WEBSITE

USERNAME

PASSWORD

E-MAIL USED

NOTES

WEBSITE

USERNAME

PASSWORD

E-MAIL USED

NOTES

WEBSITE

USERNAME

PASSWORD

E-MAIL USED

NOTES

X

WEBSITE

USERNAME

PASSWORD

EMAIL USED

NOTES

WEBSITE

USERNAME

PASSWORD

EMAIL USED

NOTES

WEBSITE

USERNAME

PASSWORD

EMAIL USED

NOTES

WEBSITE

USERNAME

PASSWORD

EMAIL USED

NOTES

X

WEBSITE

USERNAME

PASSWORD

E-MAIL USED

NOTES

WEBSITE

USERNAME

PASSWORD

E-MAIL USED

NOTES

WEBSITE

USERNAME

PASSWORD

E-MAIL USED

NOTES

WEBSITE

USERNAME

PASSWORD

E-MAIL USED

NOTES

X

WEBSITE

USERNAME

PASSWORD

E-MAIL USED

NOTES

WEBSITE

USERNAME

PASSWORD

E-MAIL USED

NOTES

WEBSITE

USERNAME

PASSWORD

E-MAIL USED

NOTES

WEBSITE

USERNAME

PASSWORD

E-MAIL USED

NOTES

Y

WEBSITE

USERNAME

PASSWORD

E-MAIL USED

NOTES

WEBSITE

USERNAME

PASSWORD

E-MAIL USED

NOTES

WEBSITE

USERNAME

PASSWORD

E-MAIL USED

NOTES

WEBSITE

USERNAME

PASSWORD

E-MAIL USED

NOTES

WEBSITE

USERNAME

PASSWORD

EMAIL USED

NOTES

WEBSITE

USERNAME

PASSWORD

EMAIL USED

NOTES

WEBSITE

USERNAME

PASSWORD

EMAIL USED

NOTES

WEBSITE

USERNAME

PASSWORD

EMAIL USED

NOTES

WEBSITE

USERNAME

PASSWORD

E-MAIL USED

NOTES

WEBSITE

USERNAME

PASSWORD

E-MAIL USED

NOTES

WEBSITE

USERNAME

PASSWORD

E-MAIL USED

NOTES

WEBSITE

USERNAME

PASSWORD

E-MAIL USED

NOTES

WEBSITE

USERNAME

PASSWORD

EMAIL USED

NOTES

WEBSITE

USERNAME

PASSWORD

EMAIL USED

NOTES

WEBSITE

USERNAME

PASSWORD

EMAIL USED

NOTES

WEBSITE

USERNAME

PASSWORD

EMAIL USED

NOTES

Z

WEBSITE

USERNAME

PASSWORD

E-MAIL USED

NOTES

WEBSITE

USERNAME

PASSWORD

E-MAIL USED

NOTES

WEBSITE

USERNAME

PASSWORD

E-MAIL USED

NOTES

WEBSITE

USERNAME

PASSWORD

E-MAIL USED

NOTES

Z

WEBSITE

USERNAME

PASSWORD

EMAIL USED

NOTES

WEBSITE

USERNAME

PASSWORD

EMAIL USED

NOTES

WEBSITE

USERNAME

PASSWORD

EMAIL USED

NOTES

WEBSITE

USERNAME

PASSWORD

EMAIL USED

NOTES

Z

WEBSITE

USERNAME

PASSWORD

E-MAIL USED

NOTES

WEBSITE

USERNAME

PASSWORD

E-MAIL USED

NOTES

WEBSITE

USERNAME

PASSWORD

E-MAIL USED

NOTES

WEBSITE

USERNAME

PASSWORD

E-MAIL USED

NOTES

WEBSITE

USERNAME

PASSWORD

EMAIL USED

NOTES

WEBSITE

USERNAME

PASSWORD

EMAIL USED

NOTES

WEBSITE

USERNAME

PASSWORD

EMAIL USED

NOTES

WEBSITE

USERNAME

PASSWORD

EMAIL USED

NOTES

NOTES

NOTES

NOTES

NOTES

Printed in Great Britain
by Amazon